Out of My Mess,
God Birthed a *Message*

Out of My Mess,
God Birthed a *Message*

Sabine Barreau

Copyright

Copyright © 2018 by Sabine Barreau. All rights reserved. This book or any portion thereof may not be reproduced or used in any manner whatsoever without the express written permission of Sabine Barreau except for the use of brief quotations in a book review.

Printed in the United States of America

First Printing, 2018

ISBN-13: 978-1-947656-34-5

ISBN10: 1947656341

The Butterfly Typeface Publishing
PO BOX 56193
Little Rock Arkansas 72215

Dedication

Thanking God for being The Author and Finisher of my faith. He created all things for His Glory including the things that seem without purpose.

1st Corinthian 1:27 (KJV) states that God chose the foolish things of the world, that he may put to shame the wise; to confound and God has chosen the weak things of this world that he may put to shame the strong things.

In my interpretation, I've found that this scripture describes God's message as something within the world that's filled with so much wisdom. That is the creature He created called the butterfly. There is a wise story which lies within the life of a caterpillar that transforms into a butterfly. My life has been a metaphor of a caterpillar transforming into a butterfly.

Just as the caterpillar creates his cocoon, I created my mess. I lived within it, and after all the mess I created, even the mess I was born into, I have seen God within my mess thus creating this message…. Out of My Mess God Birthed a Message.

Just as the caterpillar transforms into the butterfly, I have transformed into this Woman of GOD

*Lord,
I thank You because Your grace has afforded me another chance. Your mercy astounds me. Thank You for flipping the script on my mistake. Wherever You take me, whatever platform You grace me to be upon, I want to be a voice to young girls and women who are without a voice. I pray that this book will be able to reach everyone but especially women of all walks of life.*

Contents

Introduction 15
Prayer 17
   The Secret of a Prayer Closet 18
Joy 20
Growing up in Witchcraft 23
   Public Ceremonies 25
   Divination/Readings 26
   Baths 26
   Aj lwa 27
Molested 29
Pregnant; But Not By My Boyfriend 31
Self-sabotaging 37
Wife of an Inmate 41
Curse of an Abortion 45
Functioning in a Dysfunctional Marriage 51
Cancer, You Are Not God 57
34-Year-Old High School Graduate 65
Brokenness 71
   David 71
   Jesus 73
   Wait on God 74
Inspiration 80
Worship 91
The Sound of Heaven 95

Intimacy in Worship	98
The Purpose of A Broken Vessel	104
Trash Recycler	105
My Message	110
Worth	115
Restoration	121
Transformation	127
A Daughter of Destiny	130
Journaling	136
About the Author	165

Foreword

I came to know the saving knowledge of my Lord Jesus Christ through a preacher by the name of Pastor Jeffery Jean Paul. Pastor Paul was preaching revival at my home church, All Nation Church, in Brooklyn New York (Presiding Bishop Antoine Obas). This young preacher was on fire for God as he shared his testimony and did an alter call.

Now here I am, preparing to share my story with you.

Sharing my story is one thing but being transparent and sharing certain truth is what I struggled with the most. However, God has strengthened me to recount every eventful challenge I endured in order to write about them. When I look back over my life, I realize that I was sought out by God. He turned my mess into a message. I thank God for keeping me alive as a testimony to His glory.

The purpose of sharing my mess is so I can reach others to let them know that if God can find my mess to be useful, then no matter how messy their lives might be, God can do the same for them. May this book touch countless lives, lives that I'm not able to touch physically yet. God can touch through the words He has given me on these pages.

God did not allow me to die during my trials because of this moment here. He has given me the ability to strip myself and to share my story from a place of vulnerability and transparency.

God is using me as a guide so others don't make the same mistakes or end up in the same mess that I did. I struggled to be very transparent, but one thing I heard so clearly from God was not to allow shame to paralyze me or to allow anyone to hold the pen when I'm writing my story.

God put a A.G.E. behind my MESS which equals message; God is bigger than any mess I've ever created!

Mess+age= Message

I thank God for allowing my mess to become a message and not to remain a mess. My mess, mistakes, and mishaps didn't disqualify me; instead they propelled me for greater!

Acknowledgement

I acknowledge God's sovereignty. It is in Him that I live, move, and have my being. He is The Captain of my life and The Bishop of my faith.

Thank God for my husband, Isaac Barreau, who has always supported me and assured me that my story needs to be heard.

Thank God for my son, Jeremiah Elijah Vilbrun, who helped me to choose the title of my book.

Thank you, my precious mother, Jackdesse Riche, for being the first one to sow prayerfully and financially.

Thank you to my siblings for being my cheerleaders: Kevin, Janessa, Sarah, Rebecca, and in loving memory of my brother/son Melvin (My book cover is the cover of his Obituary!).

Thank you, my dear friend, Clifford Toussaint, for believing in me and for your financial support.

Thank God for Medjine Philis and for her financial support.

Thank you, my friends, for believing that my story was worth sharing.

A special thank you to all of my personal intercessors who sacrificed through prayer so I could birth this book.

Last but not least, I thank God for my publisher, Iris M. Williams, who was so patient with me during my personal financial struggle. I thank God for allowing her to help birth my first book!

Introduction

Once you get a copy of this book, you will get to see how messy my life really was. In this book, I share some of my innermost, darkest dirty secrets. Do I want to? NO! However, this book isn't about me. God stripped me of myself so that I can reach many who find themselves in the same situation or worse. I wrote this book, mainly, so everyone can know that God is still doing miracles. I am a miracle. He didn't just do miracles in The Bible days. Looking over my life, I realize that it's a miracle that I'm still alive.

God always makes something good out of the bad and something beautiful out of the ugly. For years I've been running from God because I knew how ugly my life was, but I thank God for Jesus Christ who shed His precious blood for not just the saints, but very much so for the sinners.

Before All Else, PRAY

1 Thessalonians 5:17

Prayer

Father,
I thank You for being God all by Yourself. You don't need anybody's help to be God, so I come in the volume of the book that is written of me, no goodness of my own. I come in Your strength because in You, I live, move, and have my being. Father, I need You like the air that I breathe. I need You like my body needs blood. I need you like the desert needs the rain. Father, I bind everything that has risen against my prosperity and success. Everywhere that my destiny has changed and everything that was meant for wrong turns into good. Lord, give me the power to destroy the plan of the enemy. I take back every benefit of my life that was in the hands of the enemy. I uproot every tree and its lack thereof that has been placed over my life. In the name of Jesus, I tied up every strong man and every strange spirit that has paralyzed my life; that's on my destiny.

Prayer is the most vital part of my Christian walk because that was what I struggled with the most for years. Praying was so frustrating and hard for me do. Consistently, I've found prayer to be such a big problem because I didn't know how to pray. Praying out loud was even more challenging; whenever I would start praying, my mind would start wandering around. It felt as if prayer was so complicated. My prayer life was once a rollercoaster. I had to go to the Lord and ask Him to teach me how to pray. When you pray, address your Heavenly Father.

The Secret of a Prayer Closet

I believe in the power of prayer, but I know how to pray effectively.

In 2012, I felt led to turn my shoe closet into a prayer closet; that is my sanctuary. When I enter into my closet, God always meets me there. That closet had become my secret place. In times of prayer, it's the most intimate place in my house where I encounter God. It's my altar where I lay prostrate both physical and in the spirit.

The Bible states, in Matthew 6:5-6, "When you pray, go into your room, close the door, and pray to the father who sees what's done in secret who will reward you."

So not only do I go to my room and shut the door, I enter into my prayer closet and shut the doors.

The joy of The Lord is my strength.

Nehemiah 8:10

Joy

Don't let the enemy steal your joy today. He'll try you know. You might not even realize it until it's too late. From the moment that your feet hit the floor, he'll do all that he can to distract you, to overwhelm you, to frustrate you, and to stir up worry and strife. Often his ways are subtle; other times they're clearer. It's what he does best:

Stealing. Killing. Destroying.

God puts dreams in our hearts and writes a destiny over our lives. If we trust Him enough to take Him at His word, we will find ourselves on a journey toward the fulfillment of that dream. Unfortunately, the path that takes us to the promise is always wrought with thickets and thorns. Nothing worth having ever comes easy or without opposition.

Storms will come, lions will roar, and our fears will be confronted. God allows the path to be difficult because He intends on refining us and preparing us for our place of promise. He is intent on extracting from us that which our enemy would love to leverage against us.

God loves us too much to promote us before we are ready.

As we follow His lead, we will, at different times, find ourselves in a valley – a valley of decision. Marriages die there. Dreams die there too. The flesh dies hard, and unfortunately for many, they will opt to let their dream die before they'd ever allow their flesh to be confronted.

We all have weak spots and areas of inconsistency in our character. Until we see Jesus face to face, we will need His guidance and correction. He wants to take us from strength to strength and from glory to glory.

Ephesians 3:20 tells us that He wants to do abundantly above and beyond ALL that we could ever ask or think, but there's a clincher in this verse…it's according to *His* work within us to the extent that He's allowed to work in us.

Therein will be the extent that He does great things through us. After pondering this idea a little more, I envisioned a valley of dry bones. Bones from marriages, relationships, and dreams abandoned because many people refused to die to themselves, to humble themselves, and to let God have His way in their lives.

Don't let your dream die in the valley!

If you're in a season of refining, lean in. Trust the loving hand of your Precious Savior and know that He will lead you to the other side. Refuse a sense of entitlement, and don't demand to be understood. Instead, humble yourself and seek to understand what The Lord is doing around you. He will faithfully lead you, and you will be strengthened as you go.

On the other side of this refining time is a fresh perspective and new mercies. Humble yourself under the mighty hand of God; in due time, you will be lifted up and honored before a watching world.

Here's my question for you: Do you have a sense of how God is using your current circumstances to prepare you for a great <u>calling</u>?

Out of My Mess ...

Growing up in Witchcraft

By ways of revelation, I know that I've been <u>called</u>, but not only have I been called, but God Himself handpicked me. Looking back on my life, I see my background and what I was born into. God had chosen me before I was formed in my mother's womb. My testimony might not sound like everyone else's testimony. I don't come from a Christian family. I don't know or have any preachers, teachers, or pastors in my family. I didn't grow up in church or in a godly environment. For me, it was the complete opposite. I grew up in the specter of voodoo in my home. I was raised in a family of Satanic worshippers. They practiced Vodou (voodoo). My grandmother, grandfather, mother, aunts, uncles, and cousin; all of them are Vodou practitioners. I remember I would translate for my grandma when her English clients came. Voodoo parties were a big thing for my family. That specific month, they set apart to have the voodoo parties (dans-loa).

I remember my grandmother, mother, and other family members making demonic sacrifices; especially killing animals such as pigs, goats, and chickens. They all performed rituals. Growing up, I remember I thought it was fun and normal, but once I came to know Jesus as Lord and Savior, I saw how entangled I was in witchcraft

Out of My Mess ...

and how demonic my life was growing up. I attended a Catholic church called Saint Ignatius. I was so confused because the same saints I saw in the Catholic churches were the same images I saw in my grandmother, mother, and aunties' voodoo closet. Voodoo is practiced on so many different levels. Some people do voodoo to get money, some for healing, some to kill others, and some do it to make someone fall in love with them.

I remember seeing my grandmother and mother making voodoo dolls. With the voodoo dolls, you design a doll for a person by using their name and picture. You can actually harm that person.

My great grandfather has a big voodoo temple in Haiti. That is where all the voodoo ceremonies take place. The women there would wear colorful dresses and turbans.

When I was 11-years-old, I was crippled for about 3 months because someone came to put some white voodoo powder in front of my house. When I stepped on it, I immediately came down with a really bad fever; pus and little maggots were coming out of my leg as if I was a dead corpse decaying. Every day my mom would bring a voodoo priest to the hospital because she trusted that he could have healed me and that I would start walking again. The voodoo priests, my grandfather, and the voodoo priestess couldn't heal me.

I was able to start walking with the help of Oh myrehabilitation and my cousin Yamany, who were both determined for me to walk again. They came by every day after school. Yamany would get me out of bed, hold my hands as if I were a baby, and help me to take a few steps. I was so afraid because my legs were so weak, but with rehabilitation and my cousin's help, I was able to walk again.

The Haitian Vodou Religions are full of different types of rituals and ceremonies. Some ceremonies or rituals are offered and open to the Public Vodou Community while others are conducted by Houngans and Mambos for private clientele.

Below you will find information on some of the more common ceremonies performed/administered by a Houngan or Mambo. You can click on the link to read more about a particular type of ritual or service.

Public Ceremonies

It is important to note that Houngans and Mambos do not receive a regular salary by an agency, church, or organization. Each Houngan or Mambo earns his or her own money as they work for others, help others, work for clients, etc. These public ceremonies are usually free of charge, and it is the Houngan or Mambo giving the ceremony who pays for it or bears all the expense though some of it may be divided out amongst Members of the Sosyete. However, it is considered appropriate and correct to bring a donation of some type especially when visiting a temple where you may have never attended or at which you are not a member. Many will bring gifts for the Lwa or donations of various items such as money, rum, kleren, florida water, cigars, flowers, etc. In some Sosyetes, it is common for a hat to be passed around for donations.

Divination/Readings

These are privately commissioned by clients from the Houngan or Mambo. This is one of the most commonly requested services. Depending on the way it is done, the competence of the Houngan/Mambo fees will vary from Priest to Priest.

Baths

Spiritual baths are usually specially composed for a client so that he/she may be able to achieve a particular goal. Spiritual baths may also be administered to remove negativity, to bring up luck, and to open doors of opportunity. Baths are also administered to heal illnesses.

Aj Iwa

In this ceremony, a person is married to the Lwa. By marrying the Lwa, the person is bound to the spirit and obligated to the particular Lwa. (http://vodoureligion.com/vodou-rituals-ceremonies/)

Knowledge of witchcraft threatened to take away my voice and my true identity.

Molested

At a very early age, my authentic *identity* was stolen. I lost my voice due to a very traumatic event.

I first encountered molestation at age 5 by a family friend. The second time, was by my very own uncle at age 12. The first time it happened, I was way too young to even know what molestation was. When it happened to me the second time, I knew it was wrong. I told my aunt because at that time, my mother had traveled out of the country. When my aunt confronted my uncle, he said I was lying, and I remember his mother, my grandmother, said I was lying too. I also had another aunt who didn't believe me either. We had a family meeting with my mother, aunts, my other uncle, and the very uncle who molested me. We were all there in my mother's room, but of course he denied it and said I was lying. My aunt then confessed that my uncle tried to molest her when they were young. Everyone was shocked because that was the first time my aunt ever said anything.

For a long time, I didn't like Easter Sunday. Every year once Easter would come around, I would get very depressed.

The molestation was just swept under the rug; everyone acted like nothing ever happened. We all continued to live under the same roof for about 2 years; then, he moved out.

Because of the molestation, and no one believing me, I felt invisible. This led me to become sexually active way too early. I took on the blame, the guilt, and the shame that should have been on my abusers. Throughout the years, I always blamed myself. I always wondered if there was something I could've done differently.

Now that I think about it as an adult and I've found my true authentic identity in Christ, I realize that it wasn't my fault. I was just a child that was just mishandled. I shouldn't have been mishandled. I was taken advantage of at an early age by a family member who was supposed to be protecting me instead violating me.

Consequently, I became a monster looking for love in all the wrong places from all the wrong people. For so long, I lived my life in fear, but now as I journey with Christ, I live a life of faith. I found hope in The Word of God. More importantly, I <u>found my true identity</u> in Christ. In Isaiah 61, it says, "I will give you beauty for ashes, oil for morning and a garment of praise. I also chose to forgive because when you forgive, you're also freeing yourself.

Pregnant; But Not By My Boyfriend

*"As you do not know the way the Spirit
come to the bones in the womb of a woman with child,
so you do not know the work of God who makes everything."
Ecclesiastes 11:5*

Finding myself wasn't easy. At the age of 18, a senior in high school, I became pregnant by a young man I barely even knew. The messed up part about it was that it happened in betrayal of my boyfriend at the time. My boyfriend was in jail for attempted murder because he shot my baby's father's best friend. I *wasn't* supposed to get pregnant. I *was* supposed to set him up, so they could have dealt with him due to the fact that he got my boyfriend locked up. The tables turned and I ended up messing around with him which resulted in me pregnant by the enemy!

My life at this point was like a soap opera. I grew watching soap operas like *All My Children*, *One Life to Live*, *General Hospital*, and *Days of Our Lives*. Now, here I was in a soap opera dilemma.

I remember when I would watch these shows thinking I didn't want to be like these women; trifling, conniving and cheating.

Nevertheless, in real life, I created my own soap opera, and I was behaving just like those women, if not worse.

I decided to get an abortion on three different occasions. All three times, something went wrong. I missed the first appointment because I overslept. The second time, the person who was supposed to take me never showed up. The third time, I ended up getting arrested. Four months went by very quickly. I wasn't as scared to tell my mother as I was to tell my boyfriend. One Sunday afternoon, I told my mother that I was pregnant. She wasn't mad about me being pregnant. When I told her who the father was, she was disappointed. I told her I was going to get an abortion. She begged me not to do it.

She said, "I will take care of you and the baby. You can continue to go to school, and I will support you one hundred percent."

I started to change my mind because I thought my mother was going to be so mad. She was more disappointed about who the baby's father was than about me being pregnant. My mom was very supportive.

She said, "Keep the baby; I will help you every step of the way."

That very same night I found the courage to tell my boyfriend I was pregnant.

Can you image that your boyfriend is incarcerated, and you end up messing with the guy who put your boyfriend in jail?

What a mess I created. I remember he called me very excited that night.

I said, "Hello." Then, I started crying.

He asked, "What's wrong, baby girl?"

I replied, "I have some bad news."

He responded, "What is it Elboogy, talk to me?"

I said, "I'm pregnant."

He replied, "Oh yeah, by who?"

I said, "I can't tell you who."

He said, "So, what are you going to do?"

I said, "I'm gonna have the baby."

Out of My Mess ...

So, he gave me an ultimatum. "If you want us to be together, you gonna have to get an abortion."

Of course, I agreed to get the abortion because I was so in love. I would do anything for this guy, anything just so we could be together. The next morning, I couldn't get up to go to school because I was up all night crying and thinking about the decision I had to make.

However, it didn't sit well with me. Having to choose to abort my baby so I could stay with my boyfriend was a hard choice to make. I remember calling to schedule an appointment to abort the baby. At this point, the baby was almost five months old, kicking and all. My boyfriend told his grandmother that I was pregnant by him and that she needed to give me some money to get abortion.

One week later, I went to pick up the money from her. She gave me $400 to get the abortion. This time around, I didn't go because I chose to have my baby.

For me that was the best decision. My son is about to be sixteen-years-old. He is one of the greatest and most precious gifts. I can't imagine my life without him.

As a teenaged mother who had to figure out how to stand up and rise above it all, I did what I needed to take care of my son. Yes, I had to get on welfare to make ends meet. We moved around our state a few times just so I could give him a better upbringing than I had.

By the amazing grace of God, I have an amazing, very respectful, generous, and kind son. He would give you his very last down to the clothes on his back. I watch him with the homeless people; he would rather go hungry and give away his lunch money.

Elijah is now a junior in high school. He is very active. He is in love with basketball, he loves to dance (he sure can dance) and he is active in ministering The Word of God through mime. He runs track and overall, he's a busy body.

I thank God that I didn't abort him because watching him grow is my greatest joy. He may be just one person, but to me, he is <u>my world</u>.

Self-sabotaging

My world came crashing down when I was 15 years old. Before my son, my boyfriend was my world. He was 18 and we were best friends. I was madly in love. From the moment we met, we were either together or on the phone.

Until he went to jail. That's when the destructive behaviors started.

Three months into our relationship, my friend called me and said, "I heard you are dating Cancer."

I said, "Yes."

She said, "He has a girl that he has been with for 2 years now."

My goodness, I felt my heart ripping out of my chest. I told her to let me call her back, so I could call him. I called him and asked him.

He said, "Yes, I wanted to tell you but didn't know how to tell you."

I stayed with my boyfriend without a care in the world. As long I could be with him, I didn't mind sharing. We stayed together. I knew about her; I didn't care whether or not she knew about me. However, as long as I was with him, that's all that mattered.

Come to find out, she didn't know about me. Soon she heard rumors that I was messing around with *her* man. So one day after school, we set him up. He came to pick her up from where she was working at Wendy's. I went to her job. He was with his friend, so she clocked out. We walked over to him and she asked him if I was his girl.

He said, "No."

And from that day on, I wasn't.

A thought formed in the back of mind.

I was gonna get him for playing me in front of her and his friend.

I left and went home broken into many pieces. Still after all of that, I stayed with him. Later on, she knew that I was still seeing him. At one point, we both accepted the fact that he was with the both of us. This madness went for two years; then, he got locked up. They broke up afterward.

When I was pregnant, we got back together. After I gave birth to my son, we got married. I made sure to go to school and work. At times, it was hard to believe that he had another girl. We were always together. With him being older than me, he got me into so many bad habits. We didn't care; we had sex pretty much everywhere: parks, alleyways, elevators, beaches, and one day, we had sex while one of my girlfriends watched us!

Then, he got locked up.

Even when he was locked up, we still found a way to have sex while he was at Riker's island. I loved that guy more than myself.

Yes somehow, loving him didn't stop me from hurting him. Because he denied me in front of his little girl, boy, I was determined to get him back. I did in the worst ways possible.

For years I was acting up because I had been deeply wounded as a young girl. Now, it was my time to call the shots, and I was on a roll too, just going around hurting men and some without a cause.

There are consequences to the choices we make!

Wife of an Inmate

So now, my high school sweetheart, who happened to be the love of my life, was sentenced to 15 years behind bars.

I said, "By all means, I will be by his side and do the bid with him."

I married him mainly because I really loved him and for the trailer visit every couple of months. I didn't <u>choose </u>this life, but I chose him. Prison happened to be part of the deal.

Every time the phone rang once I said, "Hello."

The operator started talking, then I would hear that I had a prepaid call from the correctional facility. I used to wait by the phone for these phone calls. Getting to him while he was in prison was tough; some said that I was desperate. I loved him enough to do the time with visits and phone calls. Letters weren't enough.

It may be a fantasy to some, but for me, it was a six-year reality. Loving an inmate is a task many can't even imagine. Marriage is a difficult task for anyone, but to marry an inmate is even more challenging.

No parent dreams of giving an inmate permission to spend happily ever after with their child, but my mother did.

As a young girl, I fantasized of my dream wedding. I had planned my bridal party and some of my groomsmen, leaving a few slots for my spouse to fill in with his family and friends. Turns out that dream was only a fantasy.

The mental and emotional stress of being married to and loving an inmate is overwhelming. When going to visit your loved ones the prison officials treat you as an inmate also. When your spouse is incarcerated, providing love and support during their sentence is crucial. Finding the strength to fulfill those duties while taking care of life's other obligations is what makes for a strong inmate's wife. It is said that the family of an incarcerated person serves time too - a different kind of sentence.

I vowed to stay committed, to write every week, and to receive all of his collect calls. I had to make sure he had commissary and had money on his books. I didn't keep a single promise.

Instead, I turned my back on him to find myself in the arms of his uncle because I never dealt with my bitterness or resentment towards my husband. I got into the marriage with the agenda to hurt him to his core.

With him being incarcerated and basically having an open relationship, I told him I wasn't going to step outside of our marriage, but I ended up having an affair with his uncle.

That was messy, dirty, nasty, and disgusting; the affair went on for a few years.

I remember going to visit him and telling him that I was messing with his uncle. I knew without out a shadow of a doubt if he wasn't already in prison he would have killed me.

I did hurt him, but I hurt myself even more.

I lived a life of many regrets and grief. I was damaged and used to walk around being very ashamed.

Curse of an Abortion

Some <u>regret</u> is indescribable.

Before my son turned one-years-old, I found myself pregnant again. This time, I was still in high school, barely able to provide my son and I with a good quality life. So, I decided to have an abortion at 13 weeks.

On January 21, 2003, I ended the pregnancy with an abortion. I cannot begin to detail the grief and damage it has caused me, and I know I deserved every bit of it. I feel as though I will always be a low-class Christian because of what I've done. I was a believer when I committed this sin. I did not do it to avoid 'disruption' in my life; I did it because I had no confidence that I could offer any quality of life to another child at the time. In my twisted mind, I felt I was doing right by the child by preventing him or her from having to suffer in a broken family. This abortion has become a curse.

Years went by, and I found it difficult to get pregnant. It was even more difficult to stay pregnant to term.

In 2007, I finally got pregnant, but at 5 months, I had a stillborn baby boy.

Out of My Mess ...

Four years went by, and I was in a new relationship. My husband and I wanted a baby, so I scheduled an appointment with my doctor. In July of 2011, I decided to get checked out.

The first test she sent me for was an Hysterosalpingogram otherwise known as an HSG. An HSG is an important test of female fertility potential. The HSG test is a radiology procedure usually done in the radiology department of a hospital or outpatient radiology facility. Radiographic contrast (dye) is injected into the uterine cavity through the vagina and cervix. I went back a month later for the results. It was then that I got the devastating news that my chances of getting pregnant naturally were impossible. Secondary infertility is the inability to become pregnant or to carry a baby to term after previously giving birth to a baby. Secondary infertility shares many of the same causes of primary infertility.

My doctor said, "Since you had three natural pregnancies previously, your chances are none naturally. So maybe, you need to look into another way of children. You can adopt or use In Vitro Fertilization (IVF)."

My question to her was, "Why I can't get pregnant naturally?"

With tears rolling down my face, uncomfortably, I heard her say, "If one or both fallopian tubes are blocked, the egg cannot reach the uterus, and the sperm cannot reach the egg, preventing fertilization and pregnancy. In your case, not only are both of your fallopian tubes blocked, but they are completely damaged."

Shortly after my husband and I left New York, we moved to Philadelphia, and I went for a third opinion. I was told the very same thing. After they got my medical records, I started to consider *Invitro Fertilization* (IVF). It was so expensive. My health insurance wouldn't cover the procedure. We were looking at $20,000 including medications. I was on the verge of a mental breakdown. Here I was unable to give my husband a child. Mind you, he loved me and wanted children.

Surprisingly what the doctor said was *impossible* became *possible* without IVF.

In 2012, I got pregnant, but six months into the pregnancy I gave birth to a stillborn, beautiful baby girl. I had fallen into a serious depression. I was an emotional wreck. Everyone who had been pregnant around the same time as me delivered their babies. I couldn't be around them for long, or I would find myself questioning God.

"Why did they have their babies, but mine is gone?"

Out of My Mess ...

I had heard and even said it to others, "Don't question God." Yet here I was questioning him all the time.

In May of 2013, I was working in a health center. For some reason, I wasn't feeling well, so my coworker said, "Go get a pregnancy test."

I said, "No, I'm not pregnant. I'm actually having my period."

She said, "That don't mean anything, you can still be pregnant."

Deep in my heart, I would have loved to hear that I was pregnant. However, I had such a fear over being pregnant and miscarrying, that I didn't care to know. One month went by, and I was feeling so much fatigue and nausea that I went to get the pregnancy test done. It showed that I was really pregnant! I went for my first doctor's appointment to get a sonogram done. It revealed that I was pregnant with twins. I was so happy. I thought that I was blessed beyond measure, double for my trouble. God was making up for the daughter I had lost with twins. I prayed for a girl and a boy, but later on, I found out they were twin boys.

During the pregnancy, I was having so many complications that I had to get a cerclage because the doctor was concerned about me losing one of the twins. At 5 months, I was bed bound. I wasn't able to work. I was home in bed. We took all of the necessary precautions, and I stayed in bed. Unfortunately, that pregnancy ended with me having two stillborn babies.

At that time, I became very suicidal. Life made no sense. However, I continued to live because I had a son to look after and provide for; still, I didn't want to live.

Losing three beautiful babies was heartbreaking and really devastating. Losing one is depressing, so imagine losing three babies back to back within a one year timeframe.

I should have been in a mental institution, but God!

It's been four years. I have not gotten pregnant. I can relate to the story of Hannah when God shut up her womb. I have been married almost eight years. I'm dying to give my husband 2 or 3 children, but I cannot rush God's timing. He knows what best for me.

I will have the blessing of beautiful children on God's watch and His time table.

Functioning in a Dysfunctional Marriage

Here I was I married for the second <u>time</u>, this time to a believer. We were not unequally yoked, so why did I feel like I married the devil himself?

We were like night and day from each other, very incompatible. I stayed in the marriage out of fear; I didn't want to be judged especially being in a Haitian church.

Their view on divorce is insane to me. The Haitian churches and the Haitian community believe that once you've been divorced, that's it for you. They already know you're doomed for Hell.

In the marriage, we both weren't happy because he felt that I needed to be someone I wasn't. I felt as though he was very controlling about everything from the clothes that I wore to the lipstick and nail polish I used. The fact that he grew up a pastor's child and also grew up in Haiti made him feel like he owned me. I didn't know that because we didn't date for a long time. We didn't really know a lot of things about each other. We came to discover things about each other's while we were already married. Looking back, the both of us had dysfunctional behavior.

We didn't know how to communicate effectively at all. Everything was an argument that ended in a fight. We were young and reckless. Once you've gotten into dysfunctional habits with someone, they can be nearly impossible to break especially when the relationship starts off dysfunctional. We didn't realize our arguing and fighting was dysfunctional behavior.

So with us not being happy, infidelity crept in. It started so innocently to me. I remember it was July of 2012 when we had a big argument. That's when my husband reached out to my childhood best friend via Facebook. He was trying to get her to talk to me. For whatever reason, they were on the phone all the time at all kinds of hours. One night it was around 2:00 am when they were on the phone. I went in the room and told him about himself immediately.

I called her, and I said, "You're my friend. I don't appreciate you being on the phone with my husband at 2:00 am."

She said, "I'm sorry, but we were talking about you."

I replied, "Right, I bet you guys were talking about me."

About two weeks later, my husband moved into our basement because at that time, she had it all planned out. She started to tell him about my past and how he was too good for me. He fell for it, but what my husband failed to realize was I had always been an open book. I was willing to tell him when we first got together. He told me that he didn't want to know, but he was willing to hear it from someone else other than me. Nobody can tell my story better than me.

She told him a couple of truths and a bunch of lies simply because she wanted him to leave me, so she could be with him. I was pregnant, and now I was faced with my husband and my childhood best friend having an emotional affair.

My *boy* even changed his number! She was the only person at the time who had his number.

When he came to his senses, the emotional affair had gone way too far. She was already sending him naked pictures and he was telling her that he was going to leave me to move in with her.

I began seeking revenge.

I went looking for her husband at the time. They were separated. I didn't know her husband, so I figured we all could play that game. However, one thing about me is I don't play fair. I looked for her husband on Facebook but couldn't find him. A year later, I remembered Facebook had this thing where it gives a few people you might know. There he was the person I had been looking for. I sent him a friend request and messaged him later that night. He replied and accepted my friend request. We were talking, but I never told him who I was.

One night, I told him the truth because he started to catch feelings. I didn't think things would have gotten that far; all I wanted was for both my husband and childhood best friend to feel the exact betrayal I felt. I took the affair to another level. I was actively in a relationship with the guy. I was willing to walk out of my marriage because the man was all I wanted. I thought he made me feel alive. Have you have seen the movie *Temptation*, by Tyler Perry? I felt like that young lady in the movie. The affair went on for about a year. I was having serious issues in my marriage from the beginning and once again I was seeking revenge.

This man turned out to be everything I needed him to be. There were some serious soul ties involved. I didn't know how real soul ties were until that affair happened. It wasn't easy ending that relationship. I remember the night when my husband found out about the affair. I thought I would have been dead or in a coma. My husband found out because I was using his phone and left my Facebook account open. The guy had messaged me pictures of us in a hotel room. That's when my husband found out how in depth the affair was. I thought my husband was going to leave me, but he stayed. Love covers a multitude of sin. We are not perfect and will never be, but we learned to love each through it all.

Does the affair still affect our marriage? Yes, it does. There are times I wish I had never agreed to work on the marriage because of how he treats me. He still throws it in my face every chance that he gets. I find myself giving him answers like, "You started the mess and I finished it."

But to God be the glory because we can talk about it now.

I know people who see us, especially on social media, assume that we are the perfect couple. Absolutely not, we have been tested by the unthinkable, but fought to stay together while others gave up.

He told me that his marriage was worth fighting for and I saw him battle for this marriage on his knees. With tears every morning for months, I saw him pray, crying before God, with my picture in front of him.

Turns out bad relationships, miscarriages and infertility were not my only afflictions…

Cancer, You Are Not God

Let me speak about my testimony and how God dried up the cancer in my body. I've been <u>afflicted</u> by the thing they call cancer not once, but twice.

Cancer has a name, and its name isn't greater than the name of Jesus. The Word of God says everything that tries to exalt itself above the knowledge of the True Living God has to be brought under subjection.

Therefore, cancer, you are not God. You are a small thing for God.

I was diagnosed with Stage 0 bladder cancer in January of 2014. My world was quickly coming to an end. I had just lost my twin boys and a month later, I was diagnosed with bladder cancer.

I couldn't catch a break for three years back to back. My goodness! Without me catching my breath, it was just one blow after another.

Lord, how much more I can take, I thought.

But I thank God because they caught it early. Stage 0 bladder cancer rarely needs to be treated with more extensive surgery. Of course, being human, I thought the diagnosis was a death sentence. I fell into a deep depression because I thought I was dying.

Thank You Father,
I give you glory!

What an awesome God we serve. What a Holy God we serve. I'm a two-time cancer survivor.

I battled cancer for about a year. When I got the diagnosis, I accepted the doctor's report, but I found enough strength to let cancer know that it's a small thing for God.

If God can walk into a dead man's tomb after four days and call the dead man forth, God can speak one word over your cancer. I had to find every scripture pertaining to healing. Psalm 118:17 suits my situation very well. "I shall not die but live to declare the goodness of The Lord."

The healing power of God has overtaken me. His Word declares that healing is the children's bread. I used to think that miracles only happened in The Bible days, but no, you're looking at one. I am a miracle. I'm a walking testimony of God's glory.

Then, in 2016, the doctor said the cancer was back...

Out of My Mess ...

I saw my hair drastically falling out. This time I was bald, no hair. Things kept going back-and-forth. They couldn't locate the cancer, but I remember God giving me enough strength to make it through. For some reason, when I couldn't get to my prayer closet, He gave me a new prayer language. I was speaking an unknown tongue. It wasn't familiar, so I felt the need to travail from the depths of my soul. There was a press in my spirit; then, out of nowhere, our relationship became a lifestyle.

Day in and day out, I thank God. I was reminded of Psalm 118:17-18. I would declare a dirty Yasha not die but live to the Claddah.

By the goodness of The Lord, I came to understand that the power of life and death is in my tongue. I spoke a life over cancer. I spoke a life over my life. I decreed a thing because The Word of God lets me know to decree a thing, and it shall be established. I established a life over my situation. I established life over cancer.

Imagine this:

Cancer has not been located after months of going to see different specialists and doctors. No chemo, no radiation, no remission, the cancer was gone.

It just shows that God is so intentional!

Out of My Mess ...

I was a medical assistant in April 2016. I was working through a staffing agency at a doctor's office. A month later, they pulled me out and sent me to work at a hospital; there I was working in the radiation and oncology department.

My God is intentional!

When I got there, I was seeing adults with two or three different types of cancer.

I said to myself, *"Oh Jesus."*

I couldn't help but give God glory when I thought I had it bad, but there were many people who had it worse than I did. I was working at a hospital when I came to a where I had to acknowledge God's goodness in my life daily!

I remember not feeling well and looking pale, but God gave me enough strength to get on my knees. I understand that death is not an assignment but an appointment that cannot be canceled. The Bible says man is appointed to die, so since death is not an assignment but is appointed, I understand that I can't push the pause button on death.

I can tell the enemy," You are not going to take me out. I'm not going to die right now."

I know a lot of people may say that is not theologically sound and that I have no control over death, but let me tell you this:

There was an old lady who came out to the temple. Her name was Hannah. She hung out with a man named Simeon, and he decreed that I will not die until I see the constellation of The Lord.

I'm here to tell you that death is really by an appointment and not by an assignment.

I had to let cancer know that I couldn't die then because of the prophecy that was over my life had not been fulfilled. I had too much promise over my life, so I couldn't die, then.

I speak life over cancer, I shall not die! I give Your name great praise Savior. If God can do it for me, He is no respecter of persons.

Whatever it is that you have going on, big or small, God is able to do all things but fail!

While we may never understand why God allows some of us to get cancer, we all can know for certain that God is sovereign and that He loves us through all of the storms in this life.

Never underestimate the power of prayer and faith.

This is the same mighty power that raised Christ from the dead and seated Him in the place of honor at God's right hand in the Heavenly realms. Now, He is far above any ruler, authority, power, leader or anything else —not only in this world but also in the world to come.

God has put all things under the authority of Christ... All glory to God, who is able, through His mighty power at work within us, to accomplish infinitely more than we might ask or think. Eph. 1:19-22, 3:20

Not only is there healing waiting for us, there is also <u>restoration</u>!

Out of My Mess ...

Father,

We command cancer to leave God's property! We evict cancer in Jesus' name! Jesus has authority over disease according to Ephesians 1, and we have been given authorization to use His name. We wear His badge of authority – The Holy Spirit that He has given us – and cancer must bow its knee to the name of Jesus as spoken by our mouths on His behalf. By the power vested in us, we destroy cancer by The Word of the Living God. Jesus demonstrated The Father's will to heal, and we seek Him for that healing now. We reach out our hands to touch the hem of His garment. We feel the surge of power that is released from His being. His light radiates through our bodies, and all cancer is destroyed. We walk in the light and receive His Holy radiation now burning through every cell in our bodies, killing every cancerous cel,l and reviving our bodies to wholeness once again.

In Jesus' Mighty Name,

Amen!

Out of My Mess ...

34-Year-Old High School Graduate

From the beginning of this year, The Lord has given me the scripture Joel 2:24. "I will restore to you the years that the locust has eaten."

I watched God make every word in this verse be made manifest in my life, restoration all the way around.

Yes, I graduated this past June. I finally got my high school diploma after 15 years. When I found out about the adult program, I made it my business to look into it and to go register because I was at a place of desperation. You can't get a job at McDonald's without a high school diploma!

I tried getting my GED 3 times and I wasn't able to. I would start and not finish. That GED course got so hard, I dropped out to continue working my *little* jobs.

To be honest with you, I had jobs for a year or more that require a Bachelor's degree to be able to work there, but I watched God be God.

I was working at doctor's office without a high school diploma, let alone a Bachelor's degree.

He will qualify you for the job. I watched Him come through every time. To be honest, for a few jobs, I lied and said I had my Associate's degree at least, but they never checked my credentials.

I remember when I moved to Atlanta, GA. I went to register for the medical assistant's program, but I needed a high school diploma to get into the program. I didn't have a high school diploma, but guess what, I got in because the administration never checked my paperwork. For some reason, they assumed that I had my high school diploma. I went to the program for 7 months straight. No one ever said anything to me, but right before they were about to send me out for my internship, they asked for all of my credentials to be sent, but my high school diploma was missing. I remember the director of the program called me in for a meeting.

When I got to his office, he asked, "How did you get into this program?"

I said nothing.

He said, "I'm afraid we have to kick you out the program because you don't have a high school diploma."

I said, "The same God who helped get me in will let me finish."

He looked at me and rolled his eyes.

Then, my guidance counselor said to him, "I don't think it's right to kick her out, not because she is done with the program but because she is ready for her 5-week internship. It's not fair because she has been here all this while. Her grades are good; plus, she is not in here for free. She took a loan out to be here. I think you should her let continue."

Oh boy, he was highly upset because he was the director and what my counselor said to him should have been said in private not in front of me. He sent me home, and the next day, early in the morning, he called me to come back to school.

God has always been with me during the darkest hours. It's not too late, but you have to want a change.

I went back to school to get my high school diploma because I felt incomplete. I came to the United States when I was six-years-old. I was getting ready to go to the State Mortuary Science Program. I needed my high school diploma in order to go on.

I encourage everyone to do what you have to do when you have to do it. Time waits on no one, so go ahead and be that nurse, be a doctor, or a lawyer; be whatever you want to be.

If I can do it, any and everybody can.

I'm a high school graduate. I have a certificate in medical assistance. I have a certificate in data entry. I have a diploma in business technology and funeral service. I am pursuing a degree in mortuary science.

By 2020, I will be a funeral director by the grace of God!

We are all purposeful. Sometimes it is through our struggles that we find our purpose. Will you allow your <u>brokenness</u> to serve Him?

A Broken Vessel

Psalm 31:12

Brokenness

The Hebrew word of Psalm 31:12 is says, "to lose oneself, by implication to perish!" Jesus said, "...whosoever will lose his life..., the same shall save it" (Lu. 9:24).

Now, what is <u>brokenness</u>?

Dear ones, will you continue in the life you have lived with its prideful and pitiful fruits, or will you choose brokenness as David, Jesus, and Paul did so that the perfume of Christ's life in you will spread beyond your tombstone into the decades, generations, and ages to come? Jesus was a broken man who took the loaves of a broken lad, and having broken that bread, He could have fed the whole world!

David

David's reputation was that of a runt: the weakest, the smallest, and the most useless creature in a litter of the eight sons of Jesse, a good-for-nothing man, but for the herding of the sheep. This drove him to God.

Then, God, overruling all the opinions and all the wisdom of men, chose David to be king. Yet, it was not long until he learned that his kingship would be other than that of all the kings of Israel. He would be a fugitive king.

First, he was hunted by Saul like a wild dog for nearly seven years, living in cold caves. Later, David was again hunted for a year or so by his own son, Absalom. David was lied to, betrayed many times, and forsaken by many of his friends who became his enemies. During this time, he also committed adultery and murder, causing him to live in his own wounds and the consequences of these sins for the rest of his life.

Indeed, hardly any well-trained theologian at that time would have given David's future spiritual prospects the slightest chance. It is highly unlikely that he would have been chosen as a good prospect for spiritual leadership by any committee. He, to them, was a wreck that had missed its harbor of success. Yet, the gospels herald him as the "Father of Jesus" in both spirit and kingship.

Despite all of this, and because of it, David became the greatest, most influential, spiritual person out of the pages of the Old

Testament. He refused to die with the closing of the age of law only to become even mightier in the days of grace, simply because he became what God wants all of us to become, a broken vessel. David was a broken vessel!

Jesus

Jesus was broken bread and poured out wine from the beginning of His life. Being totally divine and having to put on humanity to live each day amongst sin and sinners was in itself enough to break the heart of Jesus at an early age. Throughout His life, the misunderstandings and misjudgments of people toward Him brought further brokenness. Not only was He condemned for His eating manners, for the company He kept, for the truth He taught, but even His mental state was questioned by His own friends and family (Mk. 3:20-21, 31). They did not realize that the very God of Israel Himself had lived among them for three whole decades.

Jesus, The Holiest Man in human history, was judged as the worst man in Hebrew history and died a shameful, painful death. He wrote no letters. He appointed no scribes. He started no committees, and He never made a schedule to be kept. He never announced a meeting in advance. He never promoted or joined any organization, and He left behind no manual as to how His disciples were to proceed. He did everything against what human wisdom would demand for success, yet, by becoming a broken vessel, He became The Author and Finisher of Salvation for all those who believe. Jesus was a broken vessel!

There is absolutely nothing that can be said of the lives of David and Jesus to account for their worldwide blessings that continue to this day, save that they were broken men.

Wait on God

Indeed, the world is perishing, not for the lack of more Christian TV and radio programs, nor for the shortage of money given to missions or evangelism, nor for the lack of better or bigger religious machinery, but for the lack of broken men.

Oh, may I plead with you to break out of the machinery, to flee to the feet of Jesus, and to remain there until a new man is made out of the old man, until a fresh man is made out of the worn-out man, and until a man estranged to Jesus becomes a man indwelled with Jesus again.

Will you be willing to "un-busy" yourself to wait at the feet of Jesus to observe The Father, The Son, The Holy Spirit, and his precious Word? Are you willing to let the searchlight of His love expose yet unveiled carnal characteristics in your heart that have for years prevented you from hearing His voice and getting His directions?

Are you willing so to wait on God for weeks, months, and years until He is able to take out of you all the things that mar, deter, hurt, crush, and cause The Holy Spirit to be grieved?

Will you become a dead man to the self and the world to be made into a broken vessel? God can only work through those who have waited long enough to be broken. God cannot operate through people, even the most dedicated, who follow their own ideas and pursue the path of convenience. God is looking for a people who have become nothing, so He can become everything!

Consider now what God did with the broken vessels of the early church. The early church multiplied four thousand-fold in threescore years. The success of the early church can only be ascribed to brokenness, and the obstacles she faced were staggering in proportion to what she faces today. When Jesus ascended to Heaven, there were only about 120 saints who received the initial outpouring of The Holy Spirit. Let us draw from

A. M. Hills' remarkable book, "Holiness and Power," as he relates to the first generation of Christians.

Of all the ages of history, it was the age of universal corruption. Outside of Judea, idolatry reigned supreme. Gods and goddesses, representing every phase of vice, were openly worshiped in magnificent temples and at costly shrines. All power was in the hands of a magnificent and heartless imperialism. The masses were sunk in hopeless degradation, without means, without learning, without protection, and sixty million of them in the Roman Empire alone were slaves. Aged parents were suffered to die of starvation. Children were exposed and murdered. Men fought each other as gladiators in the amphitheaters and died by thousands for the amusement of the cruel populace. Every precept of the moral law was violated almost without conscience and without hindrance.

The early disciples had no wealth, no social position, no prestige, no government aid, and no help from established institutions. They were in themselves a despised and feeble folk, without influence, without skill, without education, without a New Testament, or even the Old Testament in the hands of the people.

They were without a Christian literature, or a single Christian house of worship. Pomp, power, custom, and public sentiment were all against them. They were reproached, reviled, persecuted, and subjected to exile and death. But those early Christians had the help of an Indwelling, Sanctifying Savior and the anointing of The Holy Ghost, and with that equipment, they faced a hostile world and all the malignant powers of darkness and conquered.

Within seventy years, according to the smallest estimate, there were half a million followers of Jesus, and some authorities affirm that there were a quarter of a million in the province of Babylon alone. In other words, with The Holy Spirit's power upon them, they increased more than four thousand-fold in threescore years.

Here you see broken vessels filled with The Holy Spirit, intensely in love with Jesus, whose Christianity refused to become mechanical, programmed, and tooled by anything but by the power of God. Almost every person tries to save himself. Even many of the most notable, seemingly successful, religious leaders try to save their lives and their ministries.

Jesus says, "It must all be surrendered."

Have we ever considered that brokenness may have the greatest potential for evangelism and worldwide revival?

Truly, truly, "Blessed are the meek: for they shall inherit the earth."

If there is any pride, criticism, analyzation, resentment, bitterness, jealousy, self-seeking, impatience, competitiveness, dishonesty, or love of the world in our hearts, we are not broken vessels.

We cannot find any of these traits in these three most broken men of the Old Testament.

What we want above all is the ability to respond freely to God, and all other love for people, places, and things are held in proper perspective by the light and strength of God's grace. In coming to a decision, only one thing is really important—to <u>seek</u> and to <u>find</u> how God is calling me at this time of my life.

Wind of Inspiration

Psalm 104:3

Inspiration

God has created me out of love, and my salvation is found in me <u>seeking</u>, <u>finding</u>, and living out a return of that love.

All my choices, then, must be consistent with this given direction in my life (Spiritual Exercises, [16, 169, 23], as paraphrased by Timothy M. Gallagher, OMV, in "The Discernment of Spirits: An Ignatian Guide for Everyday Living").

When the winds of change blow, I trust that God's got my back. He's got me covered. Even though I may not know the plan, God-Emmanuel, Ever-Present and All-Knowing, certainly does.

I know that I, and all of my concerns, no matter how small, are dear to God. So, I pray in Jesus's most prestigious name:

"Lord,
I do not know where I am going or what You would have me do next, but I trust that You have a purpose for everything You do and that You are leading me to where You would like me to be.

Out of My Mess ...

I ask that You would give me the fortitude to follow You and the grace to trust You even though I do not know the way or what the future holds. Send Your Holy Spirit to guide and to accompany me on the journey that You would have me follow so that my life may give greater glory to You always.
Amen."

Heaven blows like a mighty wind in our hearts and souls. It offers us a dynamic life full of energy and inspiration. When the wind is blowing in our direction, if we don't flow with it, it is useless.

At age 33, I look at myself in the mirror and ask, *"Self, if today were the last day of your life, what would you do differently?"*

This time around, God is blowing the wind of change.

The first step towards getting somewhere is to decide that you are not going to stay where you are. I'm on the brink of something big from God, on the brink of something enormous. So, I'm praying my way through:

> *Father, I thank You for strength in every area of struggle.*
> *I want to thank You for Your promise in every area of pain. I pray now Father for every person that is under the sound of my voice. I pray for guidance. I pray for divine and supernatural direction. I pray Father that I will no longer lean to my own understanding. I pray Father for those that find themselves in serious situations. I pray Father that You'll give them clear direction and clear understanding.*
> *I pray that they'll know Your voice,*

Out of My Mess ...

and they'll no longer follow the dictates of their flesh, their friends, families, or anyone else.

I pray Father that they'll be sensitive to every move You want them to make and every step You want them to take. I thank You Father for turning what has been a test to a testimony of Your goodness and of Your grace. Father help us to recognize and to realize when we are stepping into Your divine will. Father give us peace about every right choice and decision. Give them peace that passes all understanding. Use Your peace, Father to direct us toward Your will. I pray Father as we step into Your will, Your plan, and agenda for our lives.

I pray that You will grant unto us special favor, supernatural favor, ridiculous favor, overwhelming Father.

I pray that You will not only give us favor, but You'll give us favor with men. Give to Your people favor, favor that supersedes their labor, favor that gives them things people said they'll never have, and favor that causes doors to open. I thank God for there isn't anything that is outside of the realm of possibilities. There is nothing that Your hands cannot do. I thank You Father that You are turning things in our favor, especially the things that look impossible to man. I thank You by Your power and by Your hands, those things are lining up with Your will and word that it will have to open up.

I thank You Father for setting before us an open door. I thank You God for allowing me to sit under an open Heaven. And Satan, we call you a liar to your face, not behind your back. You are the father of lies, and we shall have everything God says we are supposed to have.

We know you don't like it, but you can't do anything about it. We plead the blood against you. We know there is power in the blood. There is deliverance in the blood. There is healing in the blood. There's breakthrough in the blood. There are miracles in the blood.

Fix us every sin that besets us. We pray now that You will eradicate and ease everything from our hearts, minds, and spirits. Father change our appetite.

We love because You are a heart fixer and a mind regulator. God, while we are thanking You, I thank You for mercy. Thank You because You did not give us what we deserve. Thank You for mercy because mercy has allowed us another chance.

Thank You for not throwing us away. Thank You for not killing me. Thank You for Your mercy. Thank You for looking beyond our faults and seeing our needs. Thank You for mercy and for sending Your Son to the cross.

God, thank You for grace.
Thank You for not giving us what we deserve.
We don't deserve the breath we breathe.

Out of My Mess ...

We don't deserve another opportunity, but Father, I thank You that Your mercy is new every morning. Thank You that Your grace is restored every day. Father, we are waving the flag of surrender. I thank You for rebuilding our hearts, minds, and spirits. I thank You Father that You are replenishing hearts because a lot of times we have a smile on our faces, but a frown in our hearts.

I thank You God for wiping every tear and easing every fear. We speak to fear, and we command it to leave now.
We speak to depression, anxiety, stress, diabetes, cancer, HIV/AIDS, strokes, hypertension, MS, and lupus. We command them all under the authority of God's power. We come against every sickness, disease, and plague that tries to come against our bodies. The blood of Jesus is against them all. Everything that pertains to me,
God is in control of.

He is Jehovah Jireh, The Great Provider. Anything that I don't have, He is getting ready to provide. Father, take hold of our minds. Take hold of every area of our lives. Father, thank You now for those areas that are out of control: lust, pride, arrogance, our mouths, profanity, and everything else that doesn't please you.

Take control of every habit and every addiction of the flesh. Take over our hearts. Take over our minds; take over everything that pertains to us. Help us to live in a way and walk in a way that is pleasing in your

*sight. Father, we'll give You the glory and honor.
It is in the name of Jesus I pray."*

God has taken the struggle off of my life. What was once a struggle, He turned into strength. When I say He took the struggle off of my life, I don't just mean financially. At one point, I struggled to smile and to be happy. I've learned to seek Him properly.

"I thank You Father, for no longer will I run after blessings, but blessings are going to run after me. Bless me when I go; bless me when I come. Bless in the city; bless in the fields."

I've learned to run after God, so blessings can chase me down.

*Seek ye first the Kingdom of God and His righteousness.
All these things shall be added (Matthew 6:33).*

He is my object of worship. That's why I pray every day. Not that I don't have anything to do, I am a very busy person, but I've learned to make God my first priority. You can never be too busy to seek God first. That was a process cultivated in me.

Often times, I've found myself wanting what He has without even knowing Him for who He is. Once I got to know Him more and more, no good things He has held from me; favor, blessings, and overflow.

I'm not just talking about money. I'm talking about joy, peace, patience, and understanding.

> *"Since we have been justified through faith, we have peace with God through our Lord Jesus Christ, through whom we have gain"*
> *Amen."*

I have such joy when I think about all He's done for me. When I should have died, He let me live, and for that I give God all the glory, praise, and all the thanksgiving.

These will be added onto you.

"Thank God because You are adding favor, and peace.
I thank You Father for giving to us the things money can't buy. Joy unspeakable and joy like a river, Lord, thank You for Your goodness.

Out of My Mess ...

Thank You for keeping us.
You could have thrown us away, but You didn't.
You've given us another chance.

Thank You Father for giving us our happiness back. Thank You that our joy is being replenished, and our patience is being restored. Thank You now for giving us another chance to get it right.

Help us to get it right. Fix our hearts, fix our minds, fix our spirits, and anything in us that doesn't please You Father. Cause it to aggravate us until we get our hearts and lives right."

"Devil, take your hands off of everything that belongs to us. Take your hands off of our family, children, health, and our wealth. We declare and decree now, that all things are working together for our good and for the glory of God."

Thank You God for miracles, and what was once a mess is turning into a message. Thank You God that what was a problem is turning into a promise. Thank God for turning a situation into a solution. I thank You Father for Your yoke breaking anointing. Money, houses, and cars are fine, but nothing can replace Your anointing,
Your anointing that opens doors. Your anointing can pave the way.
Let Your anointing be upon us, an undeniable anointing,
an irresistible anointing.

Out of My Mess ...

I thank You Father for we will no longer run after our blessings, but because of Your anointing, blessings will run after us. I thank You Father as we seek You, and seek You first.
You will take care of all our natural things.

There is a necessity for consistent prayer. I'm getting ready to live in houses I didn't build. I'm going to spend money that other people have sown into my life simply because I ran after the things of God, and they ran after me. I learned to stop seeking God's hands and to seek His face instead.

Gratitude and <u>worship</u> bring its own reward!

A Worshipper's Heart

Psalm 119:11

Worship

No one can teach you how to <u>worship</u>. Worship is an experience. It is to encounter God in His fullness. You have to make room for God. Worship is not a particular song. We are so programmed to the next thing. The body of Christ is always on a routine or has an agenda. Just usher into God's presence the way He's asking you to. You can't teach people how to worship.

The Bible has 7 definitions for praise, 7 different dimensions of praise, and 7 different words for praise. There is not a definition for worship. There is no song that can lead you into worship.

Worship will cause you to experience God's fullness really and truly. It's an amazing feeling to encounter God during worship. Worship leaders don't use a certain song to lead the body of Christ into worship. We are so programmed into what song comes up next.

There is no definition in the Greek, Hebrew, or Aramaic for worship.

Why?

Because worship is defined by you.

You have to have a relationship with God and be at a place where He overwhelms you. When He overwhelms you, it causes your heart to sing, and causes your spirit to surrender.

That is worship.

Worship is the true release of your spirit. It's the place of freedom that miracles happen. It's in the open place. The body of Christ has been fed this.

A miracle can only happen when you truly let go. Miracles are for God's glory. The only way you can experience God is to let go. It's in the open place that God manifests His presence. Worship ushers you to a place only God can take you to; it's when you let go that God shows up.

Walk in with a plan, from top to bottom, and the middle is God. God doesn't want your talent or your gift. He wants you.

"Lord, I will give You what You paid for even though it might not feel right, but I know You will make it work right."

"I created you to worship Me, but I paid for your heart. Stop trying to prescribe worship."

The Very Heart of a Worshipper

John 4:24

The Sound of Heaven

There are times when in my own worship space, I look for what I call the sound of Heaven. I spend time listening to different artists and worship leaders around the world, but a couple of years ago, I met this young man whose voice was really anointed.

To me, what he does is more than worship, he is truly an anointed vessel. I pray that he continues to praise God with the lifting of his voice.

That anointed voice is the very voice of my dear husband.

When I got inside the church, I said to myself, "This man is on fire for The Lord. This voice, the world needs to hear it. The world needs to hear him worship."

Throughout the years we've been together, I've heard another sound in him. He worships deeper than a song. What he does is beyond just singing.

What is worship to you?

I've worshiped for years, but after the trials and circumstances of my life, my view of worship shifted.

Now, at this season of my life, worship is for the glory of God to be moved in the Earth because in doing the 'traditional worship' people are still left the same.

We need to worship for the glory of God to transform lives. Now, I worship out of my soul.

I've met a lot of people who can sing, but to find someone to minister while worshipping is a rare treat.

The anointing oozes from the church or pulpit and into the street. It is truly an <u>intimate</u> experience!

"I love You, Lord. I worship You. I adore You. Lord, I pray that my mouth become a pen of a ready writer. I pour out my soul to You. Lord, I long for my worship to catch Your attention. The expression of my worship, let it catch Your attention. Let my simple utterances express the gratitude of my heart. My desire is to worship You in spirit and in truth."

Intimacy in Worship

In order to develop a relationship with The Lord, you have to know the <u>intimacy</u> of worship. You must know how to pour your heart out in worship. Your worship should need to be able to catch God's attention. The deep recesses of my heart are moved by Him. We can't hesitate to let our emotions show. At times, we continually suppress them until they need to be reawakened.

When we worship, all of our senses need to be alive. We should be able to hear His voice. We need to be thrilled with the touch of His hands. We have to know that He's watching us, and we have to be deeply moved by His presence.

I don't know how believers are not moved by the presence of God. When they begin to worship, there is no better place to be than in the presence of God.

There is fullness of joy, and at His right hand, there are pleasures forevermore!

Outside of His presence, we are messed up, broken, depressed, and oppressed.

Believers need to be more sensitive to the presence of God. A lot of times, we suppress The Holy Spirit. But I pray for the breath of The Holy Spirit to blow across you. There should always be an immediate response on our part.

I married my husband because I loved him, and my heart was drawn to his spirit. In like manner, I know God's heart is drawn to us individually as if there were no one else in the world.

"Lord, I will express myself to You in worship.
I can't help but to pour out my love to You in worship.
Worshipping with more intimacy, I cry out to You in worship. No longer from a place of pain but from pure intimate worship, I bow down at Your feet. I worship You on a whole new level.
I worship You from the depth of my soul."

I've come to know one of the greatest worship books. The Song of Solomon also known as the Song of Songs.

Solomon 1:2-3, "Let him kiss me with the kisses of his mouth. For you love is better than wine. Because of the fragrance of your good ointments, your name is ointment poured forth, therefore the virgins love you."

Fall in love with Jesus so much that you will be careful when you say His name.

> "Father, help me to always say Your name with love and fullness of expression. The greatest worship is whispering "Jesus.""

Just by saying His name, we are letting the fragrance of His name fill our souls.

> "Father God,
> let Your fragrance fill every area of my life. Walk amongst me as I say Your name. Whenever I worship Your name, let it be the most expensive perfume I pour out, a perfume no man will be able to duplicate. Whenever I call out Your name, fill the atmosphere with Your sweet glory. I worship You. I'm unstopping the bottles of perfume and pouring them out. So, when I worship You, I cannot afford to give You just a dab or two, but I have to be lavish and to be generous. So now, love is flowing out of the depths of my being."

Out of My Mess ...

"I worship You with words and songs of love. Lord, teach me how to worship You from the very depths of my soul. Enlarge my ability to worship and to adore You. Lord, let worship awaken my heart to love. It awakens my heart to adoration and awakens in me the ability to worship You alone."

I made up my mind never to go to the house of The Lord without pouring out the depths of my spirit to Him in worship.

*"Lord, I delight in You for who You are
not for what You do."*

Worship is a time of love. He pours out His love on me. I pour out my love on Him. I am no longer afraid of intimate worship. I worship my Beloved in intimacy!

Worship is an attitude of the heart. Worship has become my lifestyle in which my heart bows down before God. Worship, to me at this point of my life, means no one else is present, and no thoughts are in my mind other than thoughts of God. Worship is a time of love. He pours out His love on me. Personal worship is knowing God on an intimate level. It's a personal experience. I'm at a place of worship where it has to be contagious, so others will have no choice but to worship Him too. I cannot compare worship to the finest things in life.

A worshipper at heart, I'm one who thirsts for the very opportunity to be in the presence of God. I worship in such a way that I have to catch God's attention during my cry of worship. My soul cries out with a purity of heart. I pray that my praise is always genuine.

"I don't want to worship You out of my flesh. An unwavering worship, Father God, let my worship be unquenchable. Let my worship survive any situation and live through any circumstance. It will not allow me to be quenched. I worship You for who You are."

Situations change for better or for worse, but God's worth never changes and He will never <u>give up</u> on you!

God is a Trash Recycler

Psalm 113:7

The Purpose of A Broken Vessel

I thank God for not <u>giving up</u> on me. His love, grace, mercy, and forgiveness kept me. I've made so many mistakes. I didn't think God would want to use me because I didn't know anything better than to keep trashing my life.

What I realize about God is that He never throws away a broken vessel; He remolds it.

What I thought disqualified me is what God wanted to use to bless others. The enemy kept me in a jar for so long, but God had to break the jar to free me. Not only was He freeing me, but freeing so many others who thought or felt like life had already labeled them.

God qualifies who He calls.

I accumulated trash for more than 33 years of my life!

My past mistakes couldn't label me as trash because God found purpose.

My Trash is God's Treasure!

Out of My Mess ...

Trash Recycler

God is in the recycling business.

Throughout my life, I've accumulated so much trash. God searched through the trash in my life, and he recycled all of the trash that I'd accumulated.

My God is very resourceful.

He found purpose in my trash - the very ugly, dirty, and smelly things I'd thrown away. He takes what I define to be garbage and useless, and He repairs and adds value to it. I thank Him for being in the recycling business. He recycled every mistake, sin, trial, and every bit of accumulated trash from my life and gave me a new definition and purpose.

I hear the world say, "One man's trash is another man's treasure." That man they are talking about is God. He's the only one who can find purpose in trash and turn it into treasure. That is why He is known as The Repairer of the Breach. He is able to restore, rebuild, and repair it all (Isaiah 58:9). According to Psalm 113:7, He rescues the wretched who've been thrown out with the trash.

It's unfortunate that we sometimes as people only see each other as trash. God sees the treasure that's in the trash. God is a Trash Recycler and a Redeemer who reclaims the treasure that's in the trash.

My past mistakes cannot condemn me. Life labeled me. People gave up on me and thought that there was no hope, but God takes the people who have been cast aside and look like trash, and He makes them useful again.

God recycled my trash and brought forth treasure!

In spite of all the trash I've made out of my life, God still found purpose in my trash, in me.

He brought forth a treasure!

I've train wrecked my life for a long time. I don't want to go back to anything that had been a part of my dysfunction!

I thank God for recycling all of the trash I encountered in my life. When I made such a mess of my life, He came and not only cleaned it up, but recycled it.

It's so amazing that God's promise is greater than my past, my failures, my character flaws, my difficulties, and all the obstacles that stand in my way.

I used to think that what happened to me defined me, but now, I realize that what God says about me refines me.

My life wasn't easy. I have scars to prove it. I thank God for redirecting my life in a whole new direction. Everything that the devil meant for evil, God changed to good! He is so awesome for bringing forth treasure out of trash. He brings beauty from the ashes!

What a Mighty God!

I am secure in God's love for me. I am able to see through my pain to experience God's plan for my life.

God had me on His mind when He decided to turn trash into treasure, recycling and repurposing my trash. In my trash, there was a lot of nasty, dirty, smelly garbage. Where is the treasure hidden in the amount of trash I had accumulated throughout my life?

Out of My Mess ...

My mess had its purpose only to bring forth many testimonies. Out of the testimonies came forth the message. It started out as a mess. Then, the many testimonies lied in the mess.

God ended up making a message out of my mess!

God added -age (wisdom) after He recycled my -mess (trials) and what I ended up with was a message (mess+ age = message).

What I love about my God is the fact that He found purpose out of my mess. I know that God still in the recycling business, because if he wasn't, He couldn't use my mess to bring forth the message.

God caused my mess to birth a message (countless testimonies).

Not only do I have a testimony, but I am a testimony. I had put all of my mess in the trash, but God found it and gave it purpose.

My Message Lies Within My Testimony

Revelation 12:1

"God, I know You control the whole universe."

My Message

Shake off the guilt.

My mistakes didn't disqualify me, and yours doesn't disqualify you. It's not too late to turn things around.

God knows how to make up for the lost time.

I have had detours, but I will still fulfill my destiny. I will no longer sit on the sideline. I will live happy, healthy, and whole. I look and see how God cleaned up my mess. There were times when I took the wrong turn, but God caused it to be right. I have an assignment. Somebody needs what I have. I have a desire to honor God.

His mercy isn't based on my performance. He covers me in His mercy even when I do dumb stuff, even when I blow it, and even when I don't measure up. Out of my great mess, He brought out a great message. God has delivered greatness. God will bring the promise to pass.

I've come to discover the repurposed and recycled aspect of my life. As it turns out, my life experiences weren't wasted. All along,

God was recycling my trash just to repurpose my junky experiences.

It's where He upcycles and turns hopeless situations into something so much better than we could ever imagine but only when we let Him work with the trash.

When we allow God to demonstrate and reveal how our greatest disappointments, mistakes, and painful experiences can be priceless treasures, we get a fresh touch of God's supernatural power.

I have been divinely destined to accomplish the purpose of God. Nothing on this earth can stop me because Heaven has anointed me to fulfill God's destiny. I'm walking in grace and peace. I'm living in confidence in the worst of times and in the best of times. God has me in His hand. No one can move me from that hand. Hallelujah.

Matthew 12:6, I had to experience God's forgiveness.

My destiny was hidden in Christ since Calvary. Many are called, but only a few are chosen.

My mother had me when she was 18-years-old. I remember her telling me that I was chosen by God because she had a dream when I was about 1½ or 2-years-old:

I was running in the middle of the street. She started running behind me. She wasn't able to catch me, but a group of missionary women caught me. She caught up with them. When they handed me over to her, she knelt down, put one knee down, and sat me on her other knee. The missionary said that one day my mother and I would be saved.

Yes, I got saved when I was 17. To be honest, I didn't know it took prayer and confessing to be saved. Guess what, shortly after being saved, corruption began. The devil tried to interrupt God's plan for my life.

My rebellion led me to do so many foolish things that resulted in self-destruction. I had a child out of wedlock when I was in the 12th grade. I didn't graduate high school. I started clubbing at age 17. I drifted from party to party and from man to man. Over the course of my life, I was empty. I felt a void and was very unstable in all of my ways on the inside, but on the outside, it looked like I had it all together.

I remember my mother used to tell me to try Jesus! I still continued on with my foolishness. I would jump from bed to bed looking for love in all the wrong places from all of the wrong men.

Man cannot give you <u>worth</u> or satisfy you, but God's grace is sufficient.

In God's Hands, Trash Holds Value!

Matthew 10:31

Worth

"Lord, I thank you! All these years You were recycling my trash because in my trash, You found hidden treasure. I had all types of smelly garbage in my trash; not just a bottle or a can, but rotten and decaying trash.

My God is a Great Trash Recycler.

I had tossed all of my trash into a garbage heap of life, but thank God, in him my trash held value. In Him I found my <u>worth</u>.

There were times I felt like my entire life belonged in a dumpster. But what I love about my God is He never throws anything (or anybody) away. He is still in the recycling business. God never wastes pain.

For years, I sat down on a trash heap. In God's hands, even trash holds value.

My life's pain and every mistake, by God's sovereign grace, has been recycled. In God's hands, my trash became treasure.

God encases every scrap of our lives with forgiveness, goodness, grace, mercy, favor, joy, and purpose. He works all things for our good. Things in life don't just turn out well. God redeems all the bad for our good and for His glory. God is my Ultimate Recycler.

There was a time in my life where I felt useless, like I was good for nothing, but God restored me, renewed me, and used me for His service in surprising ways. What I thought was nothing but trash, God saw as hidden treasure!

At one point in my life, I felt like a waste of space. I was great at self-sabotaging. I blamed people for trashing my life. I turned my life into a landfill, and everyone else was just helping me trash it even more.

I was destitute. I carelessly placed my life into a trash can as I allowed people and life to label me as worthless, a nothing. All alone, my true potential and value were hidden in the midst of my trash. My trash was treasure in the hands of God. He is still in the business of making nothing into something. He is The Master Scrounger.

He came to seek and to save that which was lost and discarded, the wasted, the rejects, and the throwaways of society as well as the useless, the broken, and the forgotten, He is able to repurpose and to pull out the useful, reformed, and refitted. I'm not trash in His sight.

It's evident that so many of the moments I have considered wasted have turned out to be the most profitable. The things I did that seemed to be produce useless rubbish, were transformed brand new by God.

As a victim of sin, I was busy making great trash out of my life. Only God knew how to begin cleaning up the trash in my life.

I had no idea that God could make trash into treasure. That's a pretty great concept to recognize that only God can take trash from a sin-scarred life and turn it into treasure by His grace alone.

How?

God's favor looks past our trash. That's how He is able to turn it into treasure.

What's in my trash: shame, guilt, poor choices, and pain.

I've been labeled as trash, but I thank God for being in the recycling business and turning my trash into treasure. He's able to make nothing into something. I didn't like the smell of my own garbage which is why I put it all in the trash. But God overlooked my smell (sin, shame, and poor decisions) and gave me treasures of hope, assurance, grace, mercy, compassion, and forgiveness.

For years, I felt like my life was worthless and like I wasn't accomplishing anything! For a very long time, I felt insignificant, but if you were to look at my outward appearance, you would have never known how trashy my life was.

Remember, looks can be deceiving!

My worthless behavior led to shame, but I realized that in the eyes of God, I was still significant!

My past and the trash I've accumulated throughout my life doesn't have the power to diminish the value of my treasure. Only God has the power to make trash treasurable. God is able to transform the trash and bring forth treasure. I am redeemed trash. In my trash, God found hidden treasure. When I thought God was through with me, He was working behind the scene recycling my trash. He was processing my trash.

The trash process takes time, but I am so amazed by what God has done with my trash. I didn't know trash had so much significance to God. I'm so grateful that it does!

God took all my trash that sat behind the garage of my soul. I felt that my trash was too trashy and over the top. However, I took it to God anyway, and He turned it into treasure. The trash had its purpose all the while.

What messy, smelly trash sin is (fleshly cravings, weaknesses and temptations towards sin), but when God sent His Only Son to shed His blood for my sin, that's how He was able to transform my trash into treasure.

Even when I was living unattractively, God saw my <u>beauty</u>!

Beauty for Ashes

Isaiah 61:3

Restoration

The Scripture says He is going to take my difficult, disgusting, depressing, and horrible situation and give me <u>beauty</u>. He has picked me up out of the ashes from a trash pile of life and not only did He turn my trash into treasure, He made something beautiful out of me.

For years, I felt like my life was trashy and ugly, but God just needed the right climate to bring out the beauty from my ugliness. God was able to bring out the treasure from my trash just like He was able to bring the fragrant beauty of my life out of my painful experiences. Beauty was able to come forth.

Isaiah said, "He will give you beauty for ashes!"

God knew that I would be burned by life's experiences. I'm thankful that He could replace that burned out mess with something beautiful. Whatever God put His hands on, He turns into something beautiful. All I ever needed was a touch from The Master.

I came to a point in my life where there was a sense of urgency, a great hunger, and thirst. God flipped the switch on my mistakes, errors, and faults. That change was inevitable. I found myself very compelled to make significant life-changing decisions. My transition wasn't smooth. There was turbulence.

I was so used to doing worthless things that I struggled to live right, but once God put His hands on me, the transformation began to take place. God is The Greatest Coach. He knew exactly how to stretch and to push me. The beauty from ashes doesn't come easy. The ashes are the useless things in life, the very things that do not serve a life-giving purpose.

God saw beauty in my brokenness, beauty for my ashes (Isaiah 61:3).

What God found to be even more beautiful were the things I've survived. I'm beautiful not because of what I look like on the outside, I'm beautiful because of what God has done in my life. I am not pretty because of the makeup or what I wear. My beauty lies beyond that. I'm beautiful because of what I overcame and what I came out of; I am beautiful because of the work God did on the heart of me, not because of my outward appearance.

In the past, I looked so beautiful on the outside but was very ugly on the inside. God had to deal with and to fix the inner man. He was able to fix what was broken in me. There were so many things that happened to me making me feel very ugly. Day in and day out,

I would dress up the shame and cover up my blemishes with makeup, clothes, and accessories. Still, no matter what I did to my outside, it didn't change what was on the inside. God was able to mend the pieces of my life, and in His Word, I was able to find reassurance of how fearfully and beautifully I was made.

For a long time, I felt as if my beauty was stolen because of the things that happened to me. I was feeling ashamed and ugly. It doesn't matter how pretty your face looks. The makeup you are putting on your face can never cover up the ugliness on the inside. I went through so much. Thank God, I don't look like what I've been through.

At a very young age, I was sexually abused by my Uncle, and that molestation caused hurt, pain, and mainly self-sabotage. The very person who was supposed to be protecting me, violated me. I lived in a very dark place for years. I was lost and hopeless for a very long time. I hated Easter Sunday because I was molested on Easter. That molestation led to so many bad behaviors and habits. I started to have sex at an early age. If my own Uncle molested me, why not just give it up to someone else? That molestation caused me to become a monster. I got into things that I had no business getting into because I was looking for love in all the wrong places. I was hopeless.

I went through that ugly, dirty, nasty, process, and now, I stand before you beautiful. Only God could have done that. To become beautiful is not to allow the world to keep you bound, ugly, nasty, and dirty, but to allow God to restore you and to clean you up.

I was overtaken by grace from some of the things I've been through like molestation, homelessness, and sickness. My mind was a penitentiary locked up and sentenced to death, but my Lord is my Saving Grace.

Because of the finished work on the cross, generational curses will no longer follow me. Through the blood of Jesus, mercy and grace are in surplus.

The enemy has a purpose. His purpose is to kill, to steal, and to destroy, and yes, he has set out to destroy me and to keep me from my purpose.

The enemy tried to keep me from knowing my purpose, but God said my pain was birthing purpose. God allowed me to go through certain things, so I, now, share my testimony to set others free. There is purpose behind the process and pain. There is hope in The Lord.

Out of My Mess ...

When I was dead in sin, God made a way of escape. Everything that I needed I was getting through my process, but God removed that garment of shame. Yes, the process is painful. When you are called for a purpose, it creates resistance enabled to counteract everything that will lead you to the culmination of it.

God was even then recycling all of my pain. I've walked around hurting for years. I've dealt with all kind of pain. The pain of molestation, looking for love in all the wrong places, betrayal, brokenness, and hopelessness, but God remained in the recycling business.

I struggled with letting go of my mistakes. My trash was full of shame, guilt, and self-condemnation.

I can truly say only by the grace of God, my strong faith, and a personal relationship with God, I am a firm believer that God is in the recycling business.

I used to say if the pencil of life had an eraser, I would have erased so many chapters. Nevertheless, I thank God for recycling my trash, making it useful and <u>transforming</u> my life.

My Trash Caught God's Attention

Ezekiel 16:5,6

Can People Be Recycled?

Transformation

According to 2 Corinthians 5:17, even with all the filthy garbage in my trash, I had all sorts of things that God could use for His glory. God took my trashy mess and made me into something new.

Yes, people, just like cans and plastic, can be recycled too!

God made me into something new and usable. He took my broken trashy self and recycled it into something beautiful and treasurable. While I was trashing up my life, God saw the treasure in my trash.

Once we allow Jesus to touch our lives, He <u>transforms</u> our trash into treasure. God is still in the business of taking seemingly worthless lives and useless people and turning them around, crowning them with beauty and dignity.

God does not limit how much junk we can give Him. God is The Ultimate Trash Collector. All along, God was gathering my trash every day. I saw garbage in my life, but God was look through my trash. In it, He found treasures hidden.

I thank God for my gifts, talents, abilities, skills, ambition, and drive. I thank Him for doing in me the things that I could not do for myself.

I thank Him for strength. I pray that my spirit is in tune with His will. Every agenda and every plot of the enemy is being uncovered. Lord, let Your anointing break every yoke. Because of Your anointing demons are being exposed.

There were things I wish I could undo because of the pain, guilt, and shame I carried as a result on the inside. The garbage piled up in my life until I found out there was a designated dumping ground for my lifetime of trash.

God describes the dumping of all sin and garbage on His Son. In Isaiah 53, it says, "He earned our sorrows, he was pierced for our transgressions. He was crushed for our iniquities, the punishment that brought us peace was upon him."

From that point on, every sin I've ever committed was on Him. Jesus earned every immoral act, every adulterous act, and every lustful act. I've placed all of the accumulated garbage of every area of my life at the foot of the cross.

I traded my guilt for His forgiveness. I traded my pain for His healing.

I traded my death for my destiny - eternal life.

God Saw Past My Trespasses

Matthew 6:14.15

Out of My Mess ...

A Daughter of Destiny

I'm guilty of so many things, but once I tossed my trash unto Him, He then did what I or no man could have done. He forgave me and wiped my slate clean!

I'm God's treasure!

I am a daughter of <u>destiny</u>, so I must arise. I am a vessel that's been made over as clay was marred in the hands of The Potter. My life has been transformed by a divine encounter with God.

2 Corinthians 2 says there is "Treasure in earthen vessels." Back then, it was a common practice to keep valuables in clay pots. The wonder is that God made me from the earth, from clay. Therefore, I too am valuable! God is The Potter, and I am the clay. In Romans 9:21, He says this, "Does not the potter have power over the clay?" No one is more solidly in our corner than God Himself. He lifts us up. He dusts us off. The grace of God is sufficient. He took my trash and gave me treasure.

God is The Greatest Trash Recycler!

Out of My Mess ...

I have encountered more than 32 years of living and collecting trash. God has recycled it all. Only God is able to make trash treasurable. I love Romans 8:28. I don't care how bad it is for you; it can still work together for good. God is still in the recycling business. God will allow Satan to get some trash on you, but He will clean up the trash, recycle the trash, and make something greater out of it.

There is a spiritual mathematic formula that I have learned:

God plus bad circumstances equals good.

Life is often messy. God makes provisions to help us move beyond our mess. What a Mighty God, even when we make "garbage" of our lives, God can make that "garbage" useful. For example, we recycle some of our trash, but only God can recycle people.

That sounds weird, but indeed people can be recycled!

If we were to sort out all things that make trash out of our lives (lies, cheating, hurting people, etc.), we would need to stop living the way we want.

God has prepared a destiny for me without any consideration of my background, but with His purpose in my mind. What I love about

Out of My Mess ...

God specifically is the fact that He is able to turn our mess and trash into masterpieces. He accepts us for who we are.

God also downloads into our lives:

I mentioned already that God specializes in turning trash into treasure. Moreover, He can also hide Himself in us so that we always have what we need.

From childhood, I wasn't brought up in a godly home. I wasn't raised in a godly environment. As a teenager, I lived a life of a 30-year-old woman. I wasn't a goody-two-shoes. I was a rebellious, foolish young lady. At 18-years-old, I found myself pregnant by a guy that I had been just messing around with while my real boyfriend was in jail.

I had my son, and two years later, I married my boyfriend who was in jail. A few months later, I was still jumping from man to man, party to party, and job to job. My life was falling apart.

What I love about God is the fact that He went digging in the garbage to pull out the trash which was in me. He cleaned me up.

Even after He cleaned me up, at some point, I ran back to the trash with which I had become comfortable. God was so patient with me. He pulled me out of the trash again. God went into the garbage after I'd been labeled as broken, damaged goods, unwanted, not ministry material, and not good enough.

But for God, I was more than good enough. I was a treasure! He saw me as restored, precious, and new.

Yes, many people have qualified me as being broken, dirty, and worthless, but God in His infinite mercy and grace, took me as I was. He restored me to the treasure that He originally created me to be. God took all the brokenness throughout the course of my life and put it together.

God will take what may seem worthless and restore its worth. He took what was once dirty and old; He washed and cleaned it up to become new.

We all are very precious to God. He never throws anyone away, and neither is He ever done with anyone. God is The Potter that keeps molding and remolding us. He shapes us and reshapes us. God is still in the recycling business, so He never discards anything or anyone, not even me.

As ugly as my life was, I had so many regrets and shame. They alone can make everything seem hopeless, but God has a plan for everything in our lives. He offers unconditional love and grace despite our imperfections.

He offers hope where we see only despair!

A Place for *Your* Mess

Journaling

One reason I allowed my life to become so 'junky' is that I never took the time to sit down and give attention to what happened to me or how I felt about it.

I ran from my pain and in doing so, I robbed myself of an earlier healing and restoration.

God loves me, and He loves you too.

All He wants is for us to have joy and a life filled with an overflowing abundance of love. What He asks from us in return is that we honor Him in deed and service.

On the next few pages, write about all the 'trash' in your life.

Have you acknowledged your mistakes? Have you asked for forgiveness? Are you living the way you want to live? Are there things you want to change? Do you know your purpose?

Now that you know what God did for me, do you know that He can do it for you too? All you have to do is acknowledge your trash, ask Him to restore you, and believe that it can be done.

Your life will be forever changed ...

A Place For *Your* Mess

A Place For *Your* **Mess**

A Place For *Your* Mess

A Place For *Your* Mess

A Place For *Your* Mess

A Place For *Your* Mess

A Place For *Your* Mess

A Place For *Your* Mess

A Place For *Your* Mess

A Place For *Your* **Mess**

A Place For *Your* Mess

A Place For *Your* Mess

_____

_____

_____

_____

_____

_____

A Place For *Your* Mess

A Place For *Your* Mess

A Place For *Your* Mess

A Place For *Your* **Mess**

A Place For *Your* Mess

A Place For *Your* **Mess**

A Place For *Your* Mess

A Place For *Your* Mess

A Place For *Your* Mess

A Place For *Your* **Mess**

_____

_____

_____

_____

_____

_____

A Place For *Your* Mess

A Place For *Your* Mess

A Place For *Your* Mess

A Place For *Your* Mess

A Place For *Your* Mess

By recycling (or bringing forth) the trash (testimonies) that I've accumulated throughout my life, I've discovered the message from the 'mess.'

About the Author

Evangelist Sabine Barreau is a radical woman of God. She was born in Port-au-prince Haiti on Tuesday October 5, 1982, to Jackdesse Riche. She is an author and a keynote speaker. She is the wife to an amazing man of God, Pastor Isaac Barreau. She is the mother of a brilliant son, Jeremiah Elijah Vilbrun.

Sabine is the eldest of Jackdesse Riche, her incredible mother. Sabine is also the sister to gifted and talented siblings Kevin, Janessa, Sarah, Rebecca, and Melvin (who is deceased).

She enjoys being an aunt to a wonderful niece and nephews, a great friend, and is a sister in Christ to many.

Sabine Barreau is the proud Founder & CEO of Dynamic Women of Faith and Purpose, Inc. a nonprofit organization, dedicated to raising awareness for lives impacted with cancer and also to empower women from all walks of life. This organization was designed because she knew her testimony would help many. God is truly a healer; he has spared my life twice due to cancer. I am a two-time cancer survivor.

Sabine lived a life of full of experiences and mistakes. Women's issues are dear to her heart because as a woman, she walks in so many different shoes: sexual abuse, masturbation, domestic violence, fornication, adultery, homelessness, cancer, and infertility. She doesn't know how many lives God would allow her story to touch, but whatever platform He graces her upon, He will always get the glory out of her life.

"Out of My Mess, God Birthed a Message," is the author's story of deliverance, restoration, and healing. Sabine knows that if God didn't add the age to her mess, she would have remained a mess.

Sabine didn't understand it, nor did she know how. She was too messed up for God to use her, or so she thought, but all things work together for her good. There isn't any mess that is too messy for God to clean up. Her mess was necessary for such a time as this. She sees God flipping the script. Some of the mishaps she brought upon herself, and other times, she'd been dealt a bad hand...

Sabine learned to stop sleeping her dreams down. She was determined that all generational curses would end with her, and instead, all generational blessings will begin with her. Everywhere she goes she will always take her past. She is not living in the past; she wants to see how God is able to make nothing into something. He gets all the glory and honor, so her divine belief is that her destiny is in fact greater than her past.

Sabine often tells people, "Don't just see the glory without knowing the story."

Going down memory lane where her life has taken drastic turns and changes, Sabine can't help but to recall several significant dates:

- 1994: She was crippled and couldn't walk for 3 months due to a bacterial infection but later on came to find out it was due to a white voodoo powered she stepped on.
- 2004-2005: She was in a domestic violence shelter
- 2011: She and her family were homeless.
- 2013: She had stillborn twins at eight months.
- 2014: She is diagnosed with bladder cancer.
- 2015: Her little brother and son were murdered.
- 2016: Her cancer is back but is unable to be located.

Her Bible tells her in Psalm 34:19 "Many are the afflictions of the righteous, but The Lord will deliver him out of them all." Her pain birthed purpose; her greatest achievement comes from serving God.

Sabine is constantly reminded of the rough days from which strength arose. The memories are still a great part of her existence. Her daily prayer is that before she leaves this earth, she will impact and touch hearts and souls.

> "The joy of the Lord is my strength." Nehemiah 8:10

She used to quote this scripture just because it sounded good, but throughout her walk, it has manifested in so many ways. She lives by clear norms and values of life.

"She is clothed in strength and dignity; she can laugh at the days to come."
Proverbs 31:25

Contact The

Butterfly Typeface Publishing

for all your

publishing & writing needs!

Iris M Williams
PO Box 56193
Little Rock AR 72215
501-681-0080

www.ingramcontent.com/pod-product-compliance
Lightning Source LLC
Chambersburg PA
CBHW031631160426
43196CB00006B/365